BRITAIN'S BLOODIEST SERIAL KILLERS

BRITAIN'S BLOODIEST SERIAL KILLERS

From the Vampire Killer to the Crossbow Cannibal

DR TERRY WESTON

(c) 2010 DR TERRY WESTON

All rights reserved

No part of this publication may be produced, stored in a retrieval system, or transmitted in any form or by any means, without the prior permission in writing of the publisher, nor be otherwise circulated in any form of binding or cover other than in which it is published and without a similar condition including this condition being imposed on the subsequent purchaser.

First published in Great Britain by Swordworks Books

ISBN 978-1-906512-48-4

Printed and bound in the UK & US

A catalogue record of this book is available from the British Library

Cover design by Swordworks Books

CONTENTS

INTRODUCTION	7
CAPITAL PUNISHMENT	15
JOHN GEORGE HAIGH	21
IAN BRADY AND MYRA HINDLEY	29
BEVERLEY ALLITT	37
DENNIS NILSEN	45
FRED WEST AND ROSEMARY WEST	51
PETER SUTCLIFFE	59
HAROLD SHIPMAN	69
STEPHEN GRIFFITHS	77
OTHER BRITISH SERIAL KILLERS	83

INTRODUCTION

Serial killers are individuals who have a history of multiple slayings of victims who were generally unknown to them beforehand. Their crimes are committed as a result of a compulsion that, in many but not all cases, has roots in the killer's (often dysfunctional) youth, as opposed to those who are motivated by financial gain (e.g. contract killers) or ideological/political motivations (e.g. terrorists). Many times, this compulsion is linked to the individual's sexual drive.

The term "serial killer" was coined either by FBI agent Robert Ressler or by Dr. Robert Keppel (the credit for the term is still disputed) in the 1970s so that criminologists could distinguish those who claim victims over a long period of time from those who claim multiple victims at once (mass murderers). A third type of multiple killer is a spree killer. The following are brief definitions of these three types:

SERIAL KILLER

A serial killer is someone who commits three or more murders over an extended period of time with cooling-off periods in between. In between their crimes, they appear to be quite normal, a state which Hervey Checkley and Robert Hare call the "mask of sanity." There is frequently—but not always—a sexual element to the murders.

MASS MURDERER

A mass murderer, on the other hand, is an individual who kills three or more people in a single event and in one location. The perpetrators sometimes commit suicide, meaning knowledge of their state of mind and what triggers their actions is often left to more speculation than fact. Mass murderers who are caught sometimes claim they cannot clearly remember the event.

SPREE KILLER

A spree killer commits multiple-murders in different locations over a period of time that may vary from a few hours to several days. Unlike serial killers, however, they do not revert to their normal behaviour in between slayings.

All of the above types of crimes are often carried out

INTRODUCTION

by solitary individuals. There have been examples in all three categories whereby two or more perpetrators have acted together.

Serial killers are generally, but not always, male. Noted female exceptions include Aileen Wuornos and Myra Hindley.

Serial killers are specifically motivated by a variety of psychological urges, primarily power and sexual compulsion. They feel inadequate and worthless, often owing to humiliation and abuse in childhood or the pressures of poverty and low socio-economic status in adulthood, and their crimes give them a feeling of power, both at the time of the actual killing and also afterwards. The knowledge that their actions terrify entire communities and often baffle police forces adds to this sense of power. This motivational aspect separates them from contract killers and other multiple murderers who are motivated by profit. For example, in Scotland during the 1820s, William Burke and William Hare murdered people in what became known as the "Case of the Body Snatchers." They would not count as serial killers by most criminologists' definitions, however, because their motive was financial. Of course, people do things for multiple motivations.

In many cases, a serial killer will plead not guilty by reason of insanity in a court of law. This defense is almost uniformly unsuccessful. The legal definition of insanity is based on whether the defendant knows the difference between right and wrong; the level of premeditation and the lack of any obvious delusions or hallucinations necessary to successfully commit multiple murders without getting caught make this defense extremely difficult.

The United States Bureau of Justice Statistics defines a serial killing as: "involving the killing of several victims in three or more separate events." This definition is especially close to that of a spree killer, and perhaps the primary difference between the two is that a serial killer has a cooling off period. They will commit a murder and, temporarily, feel sated until they feel their homicidal urges resurface. The time period between murders can vary between a few days to several years and will often decrease the longer the offender goes unapprehended. For example, Jeffrey Dahmer murdered his second victim nine years after his first, but his last eight victims were murdered in a space of just seven months. Spree killers, on the other hand, do not have a cooling off period and are in a state of constant hunting until they are caught or killed, even though their murder spree may sometimes extend to a period of several months.

Serial killers frequently have extreme sadistic urges. Ones who lack the ability to empathize with the suffering of others are frequently called psychopathic or sociopathic, terms which have been renamed among

INTRODUCTION

professional psychologists as antisocial personality disorder. Some serial killers engage in lust and torture murder, loosely defined terms involving, respectively, mutilation for sexual pleasure and killing victims slowly over a prolonged period of time.

Most serial killers have dysfunctional backgrounds. Frequently they are physically, sexually or psychologically abused as children. There can be a close correlation between their childhood abuse and their crimes. For example, John Wayne Gacy was often beaten by his father and derided as a "sissy" and accused of being homosexual (which he was); in adulthood, Gacy would rape and torture boys and denounce them as being "faggots" and "sissies". Carroll Cole, on the other hand, was abused by his mother, who would engage in extra-marital affairs and force Cole to watch, beating him in order to ensure he did not tell his father. In adulthood, Cole murdered any "loose" woman who reminded him of his mother, in particular married women who were looking for sex behind their husband's back. Some serial killers are seemingly not subjected to any abuse in childhood, although they may have been illegitimate or put up for adoption, or just passed around from relative to relative, creating feelings of being unwanted and rootless. It is often impossible to know exactly what happened in any individual's childhood, so some killers may deny having been abused while others may falsely claim they were abused in an attempt to gain sympathy or tell psychologists what they want to hear.

The element of fantasy in serial killer's development cannot be over-emphasized. They often begin fantasizing about murder during—or even before—adolescence. Their fantasy lives are very rich and they daydream compulsively about dominating and killing people, usually with very specific elements to the murderous fantasy that will eventually be apparent in their real crimes. Some killers are influenced by reading about the Holocaust and fantasize about being in charge of concentration camps. In such cases, however, it is generally not the political ideology of Nazism that they enjoy or are inspired by, but simply an attraction to the brutality and sadism of its application. Others enjoy reading the works of Marquis de Sade, who lends his name to the word "sadism" due to his stories, which were packed with rape, torture and murder. Many use pornography, frequently the violent type involving bondage, although they may also read "detective magazines" that feature stories of real life homicide cases. Others may even be fascinated and aroused by less obviously disagreeable material. Dahmer, for example, was fascinated by the character of Emperor Palpatine in Return of the Jedi, and even bought yellow contact lenses to make himself resemble the evil character, while several killers say their fantasies have been influenced by The Bible, in particular the Book of Revelation.

Some serial killers display one or more of what are known as the "MacDonald Triad" of warning signs in childhood. These are:

- Firestarting, invariably just for the thrill of destroying things.
- Cruelty to Animals. Most children can be cruel to animals, such as pulling the legs off of spiders, but future serial killers often kill larger animals, like dogs and cats, and frequently for their solitary enjoyment rather than to impress peers.
- Bedwetting beyond the age when children normally grow out of such behaviour.

Most serial killers claim their first victim when they are in their twenties, although this can vary, with one killer claiming the first of his victims when he was 38, and another who was just 15 when he admitted to murdering four people during the previous two years. On average, serial killers start murdering people when they are in their early-to-mid-twenties.

It has been claimed by many experts that once serial killers start that they cannot (or only rarely) stop. Recently this view has been called into question as new serial killers are caught through methods that were previously unavailable, like DNA testing. Some argue that those who are unable to control their homicidal impulses are more easily caught and thus overrepresented in the statistics.

The rate at which they claim victims can also vary a great deal, and even though the US produces more serial killers than any other country in the world, the concept is not an inherently American and Great Britain is not immune to the horrific realities of serial killers.

CAPITAL PUNISHMENT

In 1999 at least 1,813 prisoners were executed in 31 countries and 3,857 people were sentenced to death in 64 countries. The true figures may be higher still. Nearly 85% of the known executions took place in China, Iran, Saudi Arabia, the Democratic Republic of the Congo and the USA.

But a major study of capital punishment recently suggested that more than two-thirds of convictions in the US are so flawed that they are overturned on appeal.

In addition, the dozen states that have chosen not to enact the death penalty since the Supreme Court ruled in 1976 that it was constitutionally permissible have not had higher homicide rates than states with the death penalty, government statistics and a new survey by The New York Times show.

Indeed, 10 of the 12 states without capital punishment

have homicide rates below the national average, Federal Bureau of Investigation data shows, while half the states with the death penalty have homicide rates above the national average. In a state-by- state analysis, The Times found that during the last 20 years, the homicide rate in states with the death penalty has been 48 percent to 101 percent higher than in states without the death penalty.

The study by The Times also found that homicide rates had risen and fallen along roughly symmetrical paths in the states with and without the death penalty, suggesting to many experts that the threat of the death penalty rarely deters criminals.

Opponents of the death penalty have used these statistics to argue for judicial reform with respect to the consequences of capital crimes. Interestingly, though, the death penalty has been abolished in the UK for over 35 years and in this time crime has increased dramatically.

Capital punishment is the lawful infliction of death as a punishment and since ancient times, it has been used for a wide variety of offences. The Bible prescribes death for murder and many other crimes including kidnapping and witchcraft. By 1500 in England, only major felonies carried the death penalty - treason, murder, larceny, burglary, rape, and arson. By 1700, however, Parliament had enacted many new capital offences and hundreds of persons were being put to death each year.

CAPITAL PUNISHMENT

Reform of the death penalty began in Europe by the 1750's and was championed by academics such as the Italian jurist, Cesare Beccaria, the French philosopher, Voltaire, and the English law reformers, Jeremy Bentham and Samuel Romilly. They argued that the death penalty was needlessly cruel, overrated as a deterrent and occasionally imposed in fatal error. Along with Quaker leaders and other social reformers, they defended life imprisonment as a more rational alternative.

By the 1850's, these reform efforts began to bear fruit. Venezuela (1853) and Portugal (1867) were the first nations to abolish the death penalty altogether. In the United States, Michigan was the first state to abolish it for murder in 1847. Today, it is virtually abolished in all of Western Europe and most of Latin America. Britain effectively abolished capital punishment in 1965

The main question, then, is whether capital punishment is an appropriate deterrent. The answer is the most difficult of all. In studying the statistics of countries that employ the use of capital punishment, one gets a sense of its ability to deter crimes. In Singapore, for example, there is an absolute certainty that if convicted of a capital offense, the death penalty will be carried out, without exception. Singapore has far fewer serious crimes, as a result. In the US, arguments can be made for either position. Between 1980 and 2000, the overall US murder rate declined by 54% while the use of the death penalty increased.

The rates for unlawful killings in Britain have more than doubled since abolition of capital punishment in 1964 and some 6,300 people are currently serving sentences of "life in prison" for murder.

So, is the death penalty the answer to capital crimes and serial killing? On the surface, the answer would seem to be yes. But, if one examines the perpetrators of these heinous crimes, it is difficult to miss the obvious sociopathic behaviours. The lack of any rational thought would mean that these people cannot adequately assess the consequences of their actions. So many of them continue to commit their crimes because they don't believe they will ever be caught. If they don't see capture as a realistic action, then logically, consequences as capital punishment are never seriously considered.

In the US, the average death row inmate spends at least 10 years on death row awaiting the death penalty while all avenues of appeals are exhausted. During this time, their sentences may be altered or commuted and the public may never know the true outcome of these changes. If the goal is to simply win a pound of flesh in punishment, then the death penalty is certainly a means to an end. If, however, the goal is to ensure that the killer is never able to harm another person again, then there may be alternatives.

The instances of serial killers are not decreasing, and the increased use of the death penalty has not seemed to deter them although other crimes are decreasing. In the end, there may be no way to slow down the evil machinations of someone with a serious mental defect such as a serial killer.

BRITISH SERIAL KILLERS

JOHN GEORGE HAIGH

Born
24 July 1909

Also known as:
The Acid Bath Murderer
The Vampire Killer
The Vampire of London

Number of victims:
6-9

JOHN GEORGE HAIGH

John George Haigh was christened The Vampire Killer or the Acid Bath Murderer by the newspapers and the case was front page news right up until his execution five months later. Nobody will ever know whether he really drank his victim's blood or whether he just made it up in an attempt to claim an insanity defense.

Haigh was born on 24 July 1909 near Wakefield in Yorkshire, the only child of a puritan coupl,e John Sr and Emily. He grew up in nearby Outwood, but his childhood was not a happy one.

His parents, members of the Plymouth Brethren, lived an austere, God-fearing life and forbade their son from indulging in sport or any form of light entertainment. They preached to him about Satan and Hell and put up a ten-foot fence around their garden to keep out the harmful influences of the outside world. Haigh would later claim that as a child he had recurring nightmares about a forest of crucifixes that turned into trees and dripped blood. A man would collect the dripping blood and offer it to him, he said.

He began to lie more and more and believed he was too clever for his parents or anyone else to catch him out. When he left school he got a job as an apprentice at a firm of motor engineers and was able to indulge his passion for cars.

While Haigh was in love with the motorcar he was also obsessed with cleanliness - possibly a legacy of his puritan upbringing - and he could not bear the oil and grime associated with working on engines. After a year he gave up the apprenticeship and took other jobs in advertising and insurance.

He learned about the financial world and did well enough to be able to buy a sporty new Alfa Romeo car. But, at the age of 21, he was sacked after being suspected of stealing from a petty cash box.

In 1934 he married 21-year-old Betty Hammer, a lively good-time girl who had no time for the puritanical nonsense spouted by his parents. The marriage was a disaster.

In October 1934, Haigh was arrested and sent to prison for fraud. His wife gave birth while he was in jail but she gave the little girl up for adoption and dumped him.

After several failed attempts at legitimate business

enterprises, he moved to London and obtained a job as a chauffeur to William 'Mac' McSwan, who ran an amusement park. Haigh and McSwan became good friends and could often be found drinking and carousing in London pubs. But after a year in the job, Haigh left to pursue more lucrative opportunities.

He set himself up as a bogus solicitor and soon came a cropper again. This time he was jailed for four years for fraud. By the time he got out, the war had started. But the hostilities made no difference to Haigh, who was soon up to his old tricks again. He was jailed for 21 months for theft and while in prison he dreamt up the scheme that would eventually make him infamous.

Haigh devoured the newspapers and learned of the dissolving qualities of sulphuric acid. In jail he experimented on dead mice, of which there were many. He discovered it only took 30 minutes to completely dissolve a mouse with acid, and thought he had found a way to commit the perfect murder.

In 1944 he was freed and obtained a job as an accountant at an engineering firm. He became friendly with Barbara Stephens, a teenager with whose family he was lodging. The age difference did not appear a barrier to their affection and she harbored hopes of becoming his wife, unaware that he was still legally married. But Haigh was about to become a killer.

One night he came across 'Mac' McSwan by chance

in a pub in Kensington. Mac was delighted to see him again and took him home to see his parents, Donald and Amy. As they chatted, the McSwans let slip that they had invested in property, which was bringing in a decent income.

On 6 September 1944 Mac vanished off the face of the earth. Haigh later claimed he hit him over the head with a table leg after being overcome with a lust for blood. But the fact that he had lured McSwan to a rented basement in Pimlico suggests there was an element of cold-blooded planning in his first murder.

He immediately went to see Mac's parents and told them their son had fled to Scotland to avoid being called up for military service. Fortunately for Haigh this rang true, because Mac had threatened to run away rather than face being killed by the Germans. To back it up, Haigh traveled to Edinburgh and posted cards to the McSwans, supposedly from Mac.

By the summer of 1945 the McSwans were becoming curious about their son's continued absence. With the war in Europe over, and the Pacific conflict drawing to a close, it seemed strange that Mac had not returned.

Haigh, who was in the process of taking over Mac's property holdings, decided he would have to rid himself of the troublesome McSwans. On 2 July 1945 he lured them to his Pimlico property on a false pretence and disposed of them exactly as he had their son.

Although he had received a tidy sum from the McSwans, by the summer of 1947 he was running short of funds again and needed another victim. He replied to an advert for a house for sale, met the vendors, Dr Archibald Henderson, 52, and his wife Rose, 41 and began to cultivate a relationship with the couple.

In February, he drove Dr Henderson to Crawley, supposedly to discuss investing in one of Haigh's inventions. Soon after they arrived, he shot him in the head with a stolen revolver. He then lured Mrs Henderson to the workshop, claiming her husband had fallen ill, and shot her when she walked through the front door.

After disposing of the bodies in his acid bath he forged a letter of authority from the Hendersons and was allowed to take all their possessions, including their car and their dog.

By the end of 1948, Haigh, whose gambling habit was out of control, had run out of money again.

In walks Olive Durand-Deacon, and unfortunately for the 69-year-old widow, she happened to mention to Haigh an idea she had for artificial fingernails. Haigh swooped on the opportunity. He invited Mrs Durand-Deacon, a neighbor, down to his Crawley workshop to discuss the possibility of him turning her idea into reality.

Once inside he shot her in the back of the head, stripped her of her valuables, placed her inside a drum and let the acid do its work. Two days later Mrs Durand-

Deacon's friend, Constance Lee, who also lived at the Onslow Court, reported her missing at Chelsea police station.

Haigh was arrested after a pawnbroker identified him as the man who had sold the jewelry belonging to Mrs. Durand-Deacon and found guilty at his trial.

IAN BRADY AND MYRA HINDLEY

Born
2 January 1938 (Brady)
23 July 1942 (Hindley)

Also known as:
The Moors Murderers

Number of victims
5

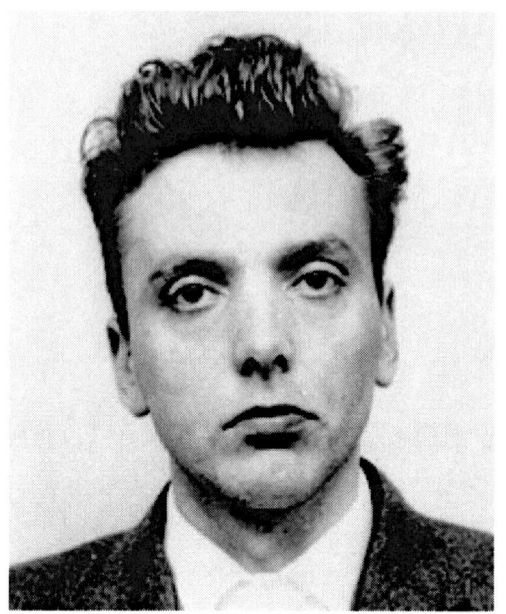

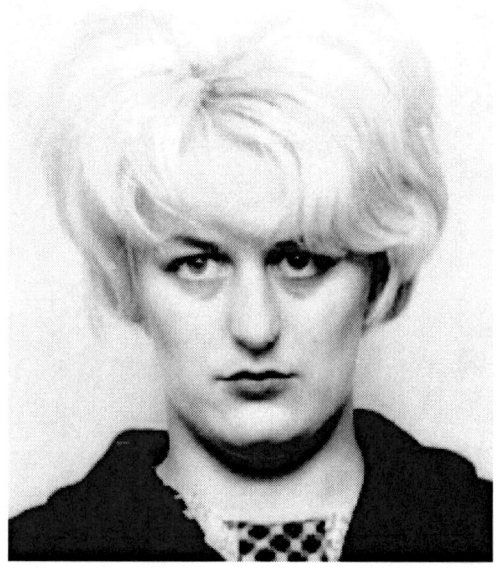

IAN BRADY AND MYRA HINDLEY

The Moors murders were committed in the Manchester area, England, between 1963 and 1965 by Ian Brady and Myra Hindley. The Moors murders are named as such because four of the victims were buried on Saddleworth Moor.

Brady and Hindley began their relationship in 1961 while working at Millwards, a chemical factory in Manchester. By virtually all accounts, Hindley was an eager participant in Brady's nefarious activities. She changed her look to match that of his ideal woman: high boots and mini skirts -- even dirndls, a word Hindley could never pronounce. She bleached her hair and the whole ensemble was created so that she would appear more German. Brady also urged Hindley to join a shooting club and get a gun license so they could rob banks.

Their first victim was 16-year-old Pauline Reade, a

neighbour of Hindley's, who disappeared on her way to a social club in the Crumpsall district on 12 July 1963. She got into a car with Hindley while Brady secretly followed behind on his motorbike.

When the van reached Saddleworth Moor, Hindley stopped the van and got out before asking Pauline to help her find a missing glove. They were busy "searching" the moors when Brady pounced upon Pauline and smashed her skull with a shovel. He then subjected her to a savage rape before slitting her throat with a knife, her spinal cord was severed and she was almost decapitated. Brady then buried her body, and it would not be discovered for more than 20 years.

On 23 November 1963, Brady and Hindley struck again. This time the victim was 12-year-old John Kilbride. Like many children, he had been warned not to go away with strange men but not about strange women. When he was approached by Hindley at a market in Ashton under Lyne, the youngster agreed to go with her to help carry some boxes.

Brady was sitting in the back of the car. When they reached the moors, he took Kilbride with him while Hindley waited in the car. On the moor, Brady subjected John Kilbride to a sexual assault and attempted to strangle him with a length of string, but it didn't work, so Brady stabbed him to death and buried his body in a shallow grave.

The third victim was 12-year-old Keith Bennett who vanished on his way to his grandmother's house in Gorton on 16 June 1964. He accepted a lift from Hindley, and she drove to the Moors and asked him to help search for a lost glove. Brady then lured Keith into a ravine and strangled him to death before burying his body. Hindley stood above the ravine and watched the murder. Keith's body has never been found.

The fourth victim was 10-year-old Lesley Ann Downey who vanished from an Ancoats fairground on Boxing Day, 1964. She had been lured back to Brady and Hindley's house on the Hattersley estate to help them carry boxes. Brady and Hindley enticed Lesley into a bedroom and subjected her to sexual abuse and torture. They tape-recorded Lesley's screams for mercy and took pornographic photographs of her. She was eventually strangled to death by one of the two; Lesley's mother always insisted that Hindley was the killer. Brady and Hindley then dumped Lesley's naked body in a shallow grave on Saddleworth Moor.

The fifth and final victim was 17-year-old Edward Evans on 6 October 1965, who was lured to Brady and Hindley's house and hacked to death with an axe by Brady. The crime was witnessed by Hindley's 17-year-old brother-in-law David Smith, who had been invited to get involved in the murder but refused. After he left the house Smith and his wife called the police.

The house was raided soon afterwards. Brady was immediately arrested and charged with the murder of Edward Evans. Hindley was only arrested several days later, when police found the pair's suitcase full of evidence in a locker at Manchester Central Station. Apart from the photographs and tape recording of Lesley's torture, there was also a notebook in which John Kilbride's name was found. Both bodies were soon discovered, and Brady and Hindley were faced with three charges of murder.

On 6 May 1966, at Chester Crown Court, Brady was found guilty of murdering John Kilbride, Lesley Ann Downey, and Edward Evans. Brady received three concurrent terms of life imprisonment (the death penalty had been abolished a year earlier). Hindley was found guilty of murdering Lesley and Edward and given two life sentences, plus seven years for being an accessory to Brady in the murder of John.

Ian Brady spent nineteen years in a mainstream prison before he was declared insane in 1985 and sent to a mental hospital. He subsequently confessed to two more murders in 1987 and has since made it clear that he never wants to be released from prison.

At her trial, Hindley was told that she should spend at least 25 years behind bars. The Lord Chief Justice agreed with that recommendation in 1982, meaning that Hindley could be considered for parole beginning in 1991. However, after she and Brady admitted in 1986 to additional murders (Pauline Reade and Keith Bennett), Home Secretary Leon Brittan increased her tariff to 30 years.

Although Brady is still in prison today, on 15 November 2002, Myra Hindley died in West Suffolk Hospital from a heart attack. She was 60 years old. Just eleven days later, the Home Secretary was officially stripped of the power to set minimum sentences. It is an indication of Hindley's notoriety that dozens of crematoria refused to take her body and the company that finally did so insisted on anonymity as a condition of performing the service.

BRITISH SERIAL KILLERS

BEVERLEY ALLITT

Born
4 October 1968

Also known as:
The Angel of Death

Number of victims:
9

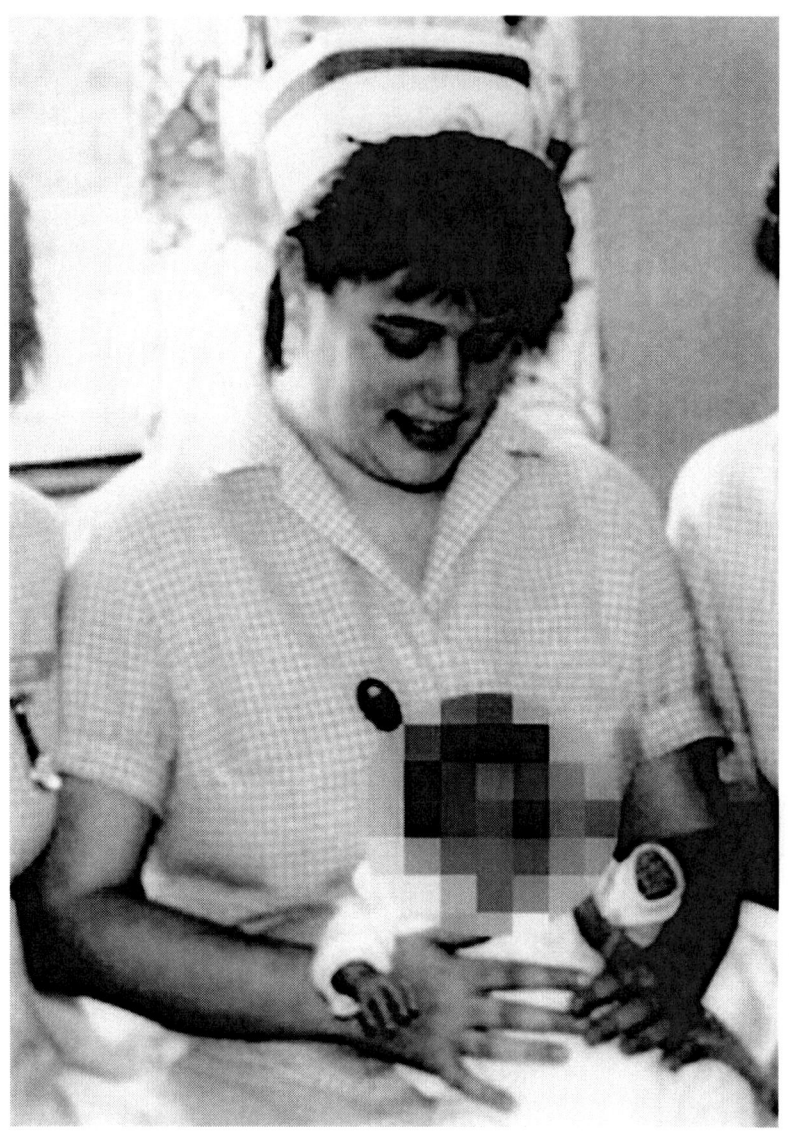

BEVERLEY ALLITT

Beverley Allitt, dubbed the "Angel of Death", was a nurse who was convicted of killing four children and injuring nine others on the ward she worked at Grantham Hospital, Lincolnshire.

As a new nurse, she seemed very attentive with the children on the sick ward, although it seemed odd that she never picked up crying babies and showed no feelings when they died. Within two days of coming on the job at the Children's Ward 4 at England's Grantham and Kesteven Hospital in Lincolnshire, Beverley Allitt, 23, took to it enthusiastically. No one knew her history or they might have thought twice before allowing her to get close to vulnerable charges.

Although she had a history of excessive sick leave and had repeatedly failed her nursing exams, she had been granted a temporary six-month position at the understaffed hospital. While relieved, she was also bitter that she had been turned down at another hospital 30 miles away in Nottingham. She was determined to show the hospital administration just how competent she was and also get the attention she craved.

On February 21, 1991, the mother of seven-week-old Liam Taylor brought him into the hospital with congested lungs. He had pneumonia but the Kellerhers told reporters later that it was a simple chest cold. Liam's father arrived and Allitt made herself available to both parents. She reassured them that the boy was in good hands and sent them home to get some rest. When they returned, Allitt told them that Liam had gotten worse. He'd been rushed into emergency care and had recovered.

Just before midnight, Liam made it through another respiratory crisis, and Allitt, was left alone with the boy. When one nurse walked into the room, she notices the boy pale with red blotches appearing on his face. Allitt then yelled for the crash team.

Logically, if Liam had stopped breathing, alarms should have sounded, they hadn't. Soon the boy suffered cardiac arrest and the doctors worked in vain to get him breathing again. Liam Taylor was alive only because of the life-support machines that kept his lungs breathing. He'd suffered severe brain damage and his parents made the difficult decision to remove their baby from life support. This young boy with no history of heart disease had mysteriously succumbed to heart failure.

Beverley Allitt watched the entire incident without a word, put on her coat and went home. No one ever asked her about her part, and she returned the next day as if nothing had happened.

Within the next two months, she attacked nine children and murdered four. Yet to the suffering families, she was an angel of mercy, someone who was always available for their needs. How could a person be so caring and so demented at the same time? Yet things were to get much worse

On March 5, two weeks after Liam Taylor died, the Children's Ward Four received another patient. This 11-year-old boy, Timothy Hardwick, had cerebral palsy. He had suffered an epileptic fit and was brought to the hospital. Allitt quickly took over his care. She was quite solicitous in attending to the boy, but a few minutes after she was left alone with him, she came racing for help, yelling that he was going into cardiac arrest.

The staff rushed to Timothy and found that his heart had stopped and he was turning blue. A specialist in pediatric medicine tried to save him, but finally pronounced him dead. It was completely unexpected. Even an autopsy failed to provide an obvious cause of death, although his epilepsy was officially blamed.

Five days later, Kayley Desmond, just over a year old,

had been hospitalized on March 3 with a congested chest. Allitt attended to her, too, and she appeared to be recovering to everyone's satisfaction. Then, in the same bed where Liam had died, Kayley went into cardiac arrest. The crash team revived her and she was transferred to a hospital in Nottingham. Physicians there gave her a thorough examination and they found an odd puncture hole under her armpit. Near it was an air bubble, attributed to an accidental injection. There was no investigation.

Stymied by this missed opportunity, Allitt struck again and again---three times over the next four days.

On March 20, Paul Crampton, only five months old, was diagnosed with bronchitis. It wasn't a serious case, but he was placed into the children's area. Just before he was to be discharged, something appeared to go wrong. Allitt was attending him when she called out that he had taken a turn for the worse. He seemed to be suffering from insulin shock, and on three separate occasions he went into a near-coma. Each time, the doctors pulled him out of it, but they were mystified as to why his blood sugar kept dropping. When he was taken by ambulance to the hospital in nearby Nottingham, Allitt rode with him, and he was again found to have too much insulin. He didn't die, but he came very close.

The next day, five-year-old Bradley Gibson had pneumonia, but quite suddenly he suffered a heart attack. The team saved him after half an hour of strenuous effort, and to its amazement, blood tests showed that his insulin was high. It made no sense. When he had another heart attack later that night, after being attended by Allitt, he was transported to Nottingham, where he recovered.

After resting a day, Yik Hung Chan, age 2, turned blue, appeared to be suffering some attack when Allitt raised the alarm. He responded well to oxygen, but suffered a relapse before being transferred to the larger hospital in Nottingham. He had come very close to dying, but his symptoms were attributed to the fact that he'd fallen from a window and fractured his skull.

At that point, Allitt turned her attention to twins, but in a bizarre twist, the mother actually befriended her. In the end, one of the twin girls died and the other child now had cerebral palsy, paralysis, and damage to both her sight and hearing.

It was the death of a 15-month-old girl that finally brought the spree to an end, and Allitt was convicted of killing 4 children and injuring 9 others. She recieved 4 life sentences in 1993. She is presently at the top-security Rampton Secure Hospital in Nottinghamshire, having served fifteen of a thirty year life sentence.

Allitt's motives have never been fully explained. According to one theory, she suffers from Munchausen Syndrome by Proxy, a controversial personality disorder which supposedly prompts its sufferers to falsify illnesses in others, in order to attract attention.

DENNIS NILSEN

Born
23 November 1945

Also known as:
The Muswell Hill Murderer
The Kindly Killer

Number of victims:
15

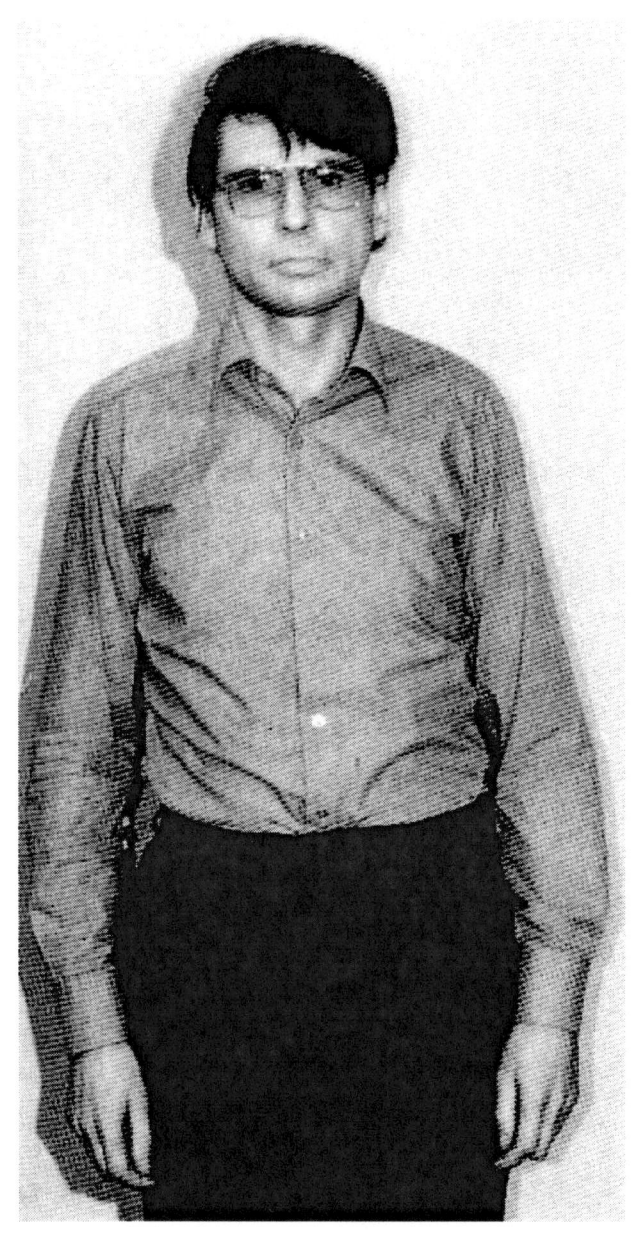

DENNIS ANDREW NILSEN

Another well known serial killer was Dennis Andrew Nilsen (born November 23, 1945), a British serial killer who lived in London. During a murderous spree that lasted five years, he killed approximately fifteen men.

Nilsen was born in Strichen, Aberdeenshire to a Scottish mother and a Norwegian father. His father was an alcoholic and his parents divorced when he was four years old. His mother remarried and sent her son to his grandparents, but after a couple of years, he was sent back to his mother again.

Nilsen claimed the first traumatic event to shape his life came about when he was a small child, when his beloved grandfather died. His strict Catholic mother insisted that he view the body before burial. Whether this incident, or his mother and stepfather's lectures on the "impurities of the flesh" helped shape him into what he was to become, no one really knows.

In 1961, Nilsen enlisted in the British Army and became a cook in Aden, Cyprus and Berlin. He left the army in 1972 and served briefly as a police officer. From the mid 1970s, Nilsen worked as a civil servant in a jobcentre.

He was involved in a series of superficial, transitory relationships with men, though they did not assuage his feelings of profound isolation and loneliness. Like Jeffrey Dahmer, he sought somebody "who wouldn't leave"; that is, a corpse.

All his victims were students or homeless men whom he picked up in bars and brought to his house either for sex or just for company. Nilsen strangled and drowned his victims during the night, waking up with little memory of what he had done. He used his butchering skills, learned in the army, to help him dispose of the bodies. Nilsen had access to a large garden and was able to burn many of the remains in a bonfire. In 1981, however, Nilsen moved to an upstairs flat. As his murders continued, he found it difficult to dispose of the remains and had suitcases full of human organs stored in his wardrobe, and plastic bags with human remains under the floorboards. Neighbours had begun to notice the smell. When he tried to dispose of the bodies by flushing them down the toilet, he blocked the sewerage of his house in Muswell Hill (23 Cranley Gardens), north London. When a company was called to unblock the sewer system, they first found the drain to be packed with a flesh-like substance. The drain inspector then called his supervisor to assess the situation; however, this was not to take place until the next day, by which time the drain had been cleared. This aroused the suspicions of the drain inspector and his supervisor, who immediately called the police. Upon closer inspection, some small bones and what looked like chicken flesh were found in a pipe leading off from the drain; these were later discovered to be of human origin. Dennis Nilsen was arrested in 1983 on suspicion of multiple murders. He apologized to the police for not being able to tell them the exact number of people he had killed. When his house was searched, they found three heads in a cupboard, and they found thirteen more bodies in Nilsen's former place of residence at Cricklewood at 195 Melrose Avenue. During the trial at Old Bailey, Nilsen was cold and distant, and seemed utterly unaffected by the fact that he had murdered fifteen people. He was sentenced to life in prison. Nilsen's minimum term was set at 25 years by the trial judge, but the Home Secretary later imposed a whole life tariff, which meant he would never be released. But after the Home Secretary was stripped of his powers to set minimum terms in November 2002, Nilsen could be freed on life licence in 2008 because of his original 25-year minimum sentence. In 1993 he was given permission to give a televised interview from prison.

FRED WEST AND ROSEMARY WEST

Born
29 November 1953 (Rosemary)
29 September 1941 (Fred)

Number of victims
10 (Rosemary)
11-13 (West)

FRED WEST AND ROSEMARY WEST

The most notable husband and wife serial killing team was Fred and Rosemary West. West was born in Much Marcle, Herefordshire, into a poor family of farm workers. He left school aged fifteen and began work as a casual labourer. After a spate of petty crime and a near-conviction for child molestation in November 1961, resulting in the pregnancy of a thirteen-year-old, he moved away from his rural home until the Spring of 1962.

He married Catherine (Rena) Costello, a prostitute, in November 1962 and they moved to Glasgow. She gave birth to a girl, Charmaine, in March 1963, although the girls father was a Pakistani bus driver. A second child, Anna Marie was born to the couple in July 1964.

During this period, West was working as an ice cream man but in late 1965 he accidentally ran over a four-year-old boy with his ice-cream van. At the very end of 1965 he, Anna McFall and Rena West moved to Gloucester, and West took a job in an abattoir. Their marriage under strain, the Wests separated, and when she returned in 1966, he was living with Anna McFall. West killed the heavily pregnant McFall around August 1967 and buried her in a field near Much Marcle. Rena returned to live with him and their children for a short time before leaving again.

In late 1968, West met Rosemary Letts (b. 1953). She became pregnant and left her family home to move in with West in Midland Road in Gloucester. She gave birth to a girl, Heather, on 17 October 1970, and often neglected the older children. Charmaine died in mid-1971 while West was still in prison, probably at Letts' hands. West dismembered the body upon returning from prison, and hid it under the floor. Rena returned to Gloucester in late August 1971 looking for her children. West murdered her one night after she was drunk and disposed of the body near his childhood home. He committed Bigamy by marrying Rosemary Letts on 29 January 1972, but West regularly encouraged Rose to prostitute herself. Rose gave birth to a girl, Mae, in June 1972, and the family moved to a new home at 25 Cromwell Street, an unprepossessing three-story house.

West adapted the cellar as a place for his wife to work, extending and soundproofing it. It was there that West raped 17-year-old Caroline Owens, whom they had taken in as a nanny, in late 1972. West was arrested and went to trial in January 1973, but he was only fined. West then began following a pattern: young females would come to their home as lodgers or to care for the children and would be abused and then murdered. The first victim was Lynda Gough, murdered shortly after West's trial. The second was 15-year old Carol Ann Cooper, abducted and murdered around November 1973, and the third was Lucy Partington (a relative of Martin Amis), murdered in January 1974. The bodies were dismembered and disposed of under the cellar floor as West extended and renovated the building.

Lucy Partington, Therese Siegenthaler, Carol Cooper, Juanita Mott and Shirley Hubbard were murdered from 1973 to 1975. They were all buried under the cellar floor. There was a hiatus before Shirley Robinson, a pregnant ex-prostitute, was murdered in May 1978 and buried in the garden. In August 1979 the Wests abducted, abused, tortured and killed Alison Chambers.

Rose was often pregnant, and gave birth to Tara (December 1977), Louise (November 1978), Barry (June 1980), Rosemary Junior (April 1982) and Lucyanna (July 1983). Tara, Rosemary and Lucyanna were not West's children.

If the Wests continued their behaviour after killing Chambers and Siegenthaler, they did not conceal the bodies in the house. The next woman to be buried at Cromwell Street was West's daughter Heather. She was murdered and buried in the garden in June 1987.

Following the report of the rape of West's 13-year-old daughter in May and June 1992, police obtained a search warrant. After examining the house, they arrested West for rape and sodomy of a minor and Rose as an accomplice on 6 August 1992. She was also charged with Child cruelty. Police interviewed the West's children, discovering the abuse and the mysterious disappearances of Charmaine, Heather and Rena. The six surviving children still at home were taken into care.

The rape case against West collapsed when the two main witnesses declined to testify on 7 June 1993. However, the police obtained a further search warrant in February 1994, allowing them to excavate the garden in search of Heather. The police began searching the house and excavating the garden on February 24, 1994. On the 25th, after the police had uncovered human bones, West confessed, retracted and then re-confessed to the murder of his daughter, denying that Rose was involved. Rose was not arrested until April 1994, initially only on sex offenses. The extended search and the grisly finds prompted much media interest.

On 30 June 1994, they appeared in the dock in Gloucester, the first time they had seen each other since 25 February, when Fred was arrested for the murder of Heather. He attempted to touch Rose in the dock to console her but she totally ignored him. Outside, Fred West was arrested on suspicion of murdering Anna McFall, whose body was found on 7 June 1994. On the evening 3 July 1994 he was charged with her murder.

On December 13 1994, West was charged with twelve murders. His wife ten. She ignored him a second time, and on January 1, 1995, he committed suicide in his cell at Birmingham's Winson Green Prison. The evidence against Rose was largely circumstantial, and she did not confess. She was tried from October 1995, found guilty of ten murders and sentenced to life imprisonment. A whole life tariff was imposed on her, and she is extremely unlikely to be released.

In October 1996, the Wests' home was demolished, and the site became a simple pathway.

BRITISH SERIAL KILLERS

PETER SUTCLIFFE

Born
2 June 1946

Also known as:
The Yorkshire Ripper

Number of victims:
13

PETER WILLIAM SUTCLIFFE

Peter William Sutcliffe was infamous as the "Yorkshire Ripper", and convicted in 1981 of the murders of thirteen women and attacks on seven more from 1975 to 1980.

Sutcliffe was born in Bingley, West Yorkshire, the son of a mill-worker. Reportedly a loner at school, he left formal education at the age of fifteen and took a series of menial jobs, including a stint as a grave-digger, before settling into a job on the nightshift at a local factory.

He met Sonia Szurma in 1966, and they married in 1974. After several miscarriages, Sonia went back to school, and when she completed the course in 1977 and began teaching, the couple used the extra money to buy their first house, in Bradford.

The first known assault by Sutcliffe was in Keighley on 5 July, 1975. He attacked Anna Rogulskyj (aged 36), who was walking alone, striking her unconscious with a ball-peen hammer and slashing her stomach with a knife. Disturbed by a neighbour, he left without killing her. Sutcliffe attacked Olive Smelt (aged 46) in Halifax in August with the same MO and again was disturbed and left his victim badly injured. Later in August, he attacked Tracy Browne (aged 16) in Silsden. She was struck from behind and hit on the head five times while walking in a country lane. Sutcliffe was not convicted of this attack, but later confessed to it.

His next victim, Wilma McCann of Leeds (aged 28) and a mother of four, was killed on 30 October. He struck her twice with a hammer before stabbing her fifteen times. An extensive inquiry, involving 150 police officers and 11,000 interviews, did not uncover Sutcliffe.

He did not kill again until January 1976, stabbing Emily Jackson (aged 42) 51 times in Leeds.

Due to repeated absenteeism, Sutcliffe lost his first driving job in March 1976 and did not find another until October. He attacked Marcella Claxton (aged 20), another prostitute, in Roundhay Park in Leeds on 9 May. He struck her with a hammer and left her with 25 stab wounds.

The next murder took place in February 1977. He attacked Irene Richardson (aged 28), another Chapeltown prostitute, in Roundhay Park, this time killing her with a series of weighty hammer blows, followed by a postmortem stabbing.

Two months later he killed Patricia "Tina" Atkinson (aged 32), a Bradford prostitute, at her flat, where police found a bootprint on the bedclothes. 2 months later, his crimes escalated with the vicious murder in Chapeltown of Jayne MacDonald (aged 16) who was not a prostitute, and in the public perception, her death suddenly made every woman a potential victim. He seriously assaulted Maureen Long (aged 42) in Bradford in July; and left her for dead. He was seen by a witness, but the make of his car was misidentified. The police had over 300 officers working the case and amassed 12,500 statements without result.

Sutcliffe killed Manchester prostitute Jean Jordan (aged 20) in October. Her body was not found for ten days, but had obviously been moved several days after death. The recovery of her handbag offered a valuable piece of evidence. Sutcliffe had given the woman £5. The note was new and was traced to banks in Shipley and Bingley and from there into the wages of 8,000 local employees. Over three months the police interviewed 5,000 men, including Sutcliffe, but did not connect him. Sutcliffe had known the note could expose him: he had returned to the body a week after the killing to locate it and, unable to find the handbag, had tried to remove Jordan's head with a broken pane of glass and a hacksaw. Chillingly, he had undertaken this event after hosting a family party at his home. Jordan's body was discovered by Bruce Jones, who later went on to play the part of Les Battersby in the long-running TV soap opera Coronation Street.

Sutcliffe attacked another Leeds prostitute, Marilyn Moore (aged 25) in December. She survived and offered another reasonable description of her attacker, and tire tracks found matched those of an earlier attack.

Despite this, the police withdrew their intensive search for the person who received the £5 in January 1978. Sutcliffe was interviewed about the £5 note, but not investigated further; he would ultimately be contacted, and disregarded, by the Ripper Squad many more times. In that month, Sutcliffe killed another Bradford prostitute, Yvonne Pearson (aged 21), this time hiding the body under a discarded sofa so that it was not found until March. Undeterred, he killed Huddersfield prostitute, Helen Rytka (aged 18), in late January; her body was uncovered three days later.

After a two-month hiatus Sutcliffe killed again, attacking Vera Millward (aged 40) in the car park of the Manchester Royal Infirmary on 16 May.

Almost a year passed before he struck again; during this time his mother died. On 4 April, 1979, he killed Josephine Whitaker (aged 19), a bank clerk, in Halifax; he assaulted her on the town moor as she was walking home. Despite new forensic clues, the police efforts were diverted for several months into a fruitless search for a man with a Wearside accent, which was pinned down to the Castletown area of Sunderland, following a hoax tape message taunting Superintendent George Oldfield, who was leading the search. The same hoaxer had sent two letters to the police boasting of his crimes in 1978 signed "Jack The Ripper" and claimed a murder (that of 26-year-old Joan Harrison) in Preston in November 1975. On 20 October, 2005, John Humble, an unemployed alcoholic and long-time resident of the Ford Estate area of Sunderland (a mile away from Castletown), was charged with attempting to pervert the course of justice in response to the sending of the hoax letters and tape, and remanded in custody. On March 21, 2006 he was sentenced to eight years in prison. It is expected that he will also be questioned in connection with the Harrison murder.

Sutcliffe killed Barbara Leach (aged 20), a Bradford student, in September, his sixteenth attack. Yet again the murder of a woman who was not a prostitute aroused the public and prompted an expensive publicity campaign, which unfortunately pushed the Wearside connection. Even with this false lead, Sutcliffe was re-interviewed on at least two occasions in 1979, but despite matching several forensic clues and being on the list of just 300 names in connection with the £5 note, he was not strongly suspected. In total, Sutcliffe was interviewed by the police on nine occasions.

In April 1980 he was arrested for drunken driving. While awaiting trial on this charge he killed two more women, Marguerite Walls (aged 47) in August and Jacqueline Hill (aged 20) in November 1980. He also attacked two other women who survived – Upadhya Bandara (aged 34) in Leeds and Theresa Sykes (aged 16) in Huddersfield. Following the November murder, one of Sutcliffe's friends reported him to the police as a suspect; this information vanished into the enormous volumes already created.

In January 1981 he was stopped by the police in the driveway of Light Trades House on Melbourne Avenue in Broomhill, Sheffield, South Yorkshire while in his car with prostitute Olivia Reivers (aged 24); he was arrested, on grounds of having fitted his car with false number plates. He was transferred to Dewsbury police station in connection with this offence. At Dewsbury he was questioned in relation to the Yorkshire Ripper case, as he matched so many of the physical characteristics known. The discovery the next day of a knife, hammer and rope he had disposed of at the time and place of his arrest along Melbourne Avenue (he used the pretext of needing to urinate to absent himself briefly from the arresting officers) increased police interest, and they obtained a search warrant for his home and brought his wife in for questioning.

After two days of intensive questioning, he suddenly

declared he was the Ripper and, over the next day, calmly described his many attacks, only weeks later claiming to have been told by God to murder the women. He was charged on 6 January and went to trial in May.

The basis of his defence was his claim that he was the tool of God's will. However, there was a twist to the tale that, had it been made public at the time, could have shattered this defence, and exposed Sutcliffe as the sexual killer many believed he was. When Sutcliffe stripped out of his clothing at the police station, he was discovered to be wearing a V-neck pullover under his trousers. The arms had been pulled over his legs, so that the V-neck exposed his groin; the elbows were padded to protect his knees as, presumably, he knelt over his victims' corpses. The sexual implications of this outfit were held to be obvious.

His trial lasted just two weeks; he was found guilty of thirteen counts of murder and was sentenced to life imprisonment with a recommendation that he serve a minimum of thirty years. His appeal was denied. Since his incarceration, he has been informed that he will die a prisoner.

HAROLD SHIPMAN

Born
14 January 1946(1946-01-14)

Also known as:
Dr Death

Number of victims
215+

HAROLD FREDERICK "FRED" SHIPMAN

Harold Frederick Shipman was a British general practitioner who was the most prolific known serial killer in the history of Britain (and possibly the world).

He killed around 250 patients from the 1970s to 1998, in Hyde, Greater Manchester, mainly elderly women who lived alone and were otherwise in good health. He was eventually caught after he ineptly forged a new will in the name of one of his victims. He was convicted on 15 sample charges in 2000 and sentenced to life imprisonment. He committed suicide in 2004 at HMP Wakefield, West Yorkshire, without admitting to or explaining his crimes.

Shipman was born in Nottingham, the second of three children, and was known as Fred or Freddy to his family. His mother, Vera, died in 1963 from lung cancer, when he was 17. He went to University of Leeds medical school in 1965, and around this time, he met his future wife,

Primrose (who was three years his junior).

They married in 1966, and Primrose gave birth to their first child, Sarah, four months later. In tota,l they had four children. In 1970, he graduated from Leeds and started work at Pontefract General Infirmary in Pontefract, a small town southeast of Leeds. It was apparently here that he started murdering people.

In 1974, Shipman took his first GP position in Todmorden, 12.5 miles west of Halifax, West Yorkshire. Soon after this, in 1975 he was caught forging prescriptions of pethidine for his own use. Sent briefly to a drug rehabilitation clinic in York, he was pronounced clean, and became a GP at the Donneybrook Medical Centre in Hyde, Tameside, Greater Manchester in 1977.

Shipman continued working as a GP in Hyde throughout the 1980s, founding a clinic of his own in 1993, on Market Street. He became a respected member of the community.

In March 1998, Dr. Linda Reynolds of the Brooke Surgery in Hyde, opposite Shipman's clinic, went to John Pollard, the coroner for the South Manchester district, with concerns about the high death rate among Shipman's patients (in particular the large number of cremation forms for elderly women that he had needed countersigning).

She said that he was "killing" his patients, although she was not sure whether it was malpractice or malice. The matter was brought to the attention of the police, who were unable to find sufficient evidence to bring charges. (The Shipman Inquiry later apportioned blame on the police for assigning inexperienced officers to the case.) Between the time the investigation was abandoned on April 17, and Shipman's eventual arrest, he had killed a further three people.

The last of these was Kathleen Grundy, a former Mayor of Hyde. On 24 June 1998, she was found dead at her home. The last person to see her alive had been Shipman, who later signed her death certificate.

Grundy's daughter, lawyer Angela Woodruff, became concerned when she discovered that a will had been made, apparently by her mother, which excluded her entirely and bequeathed £386,000 to Shipman. Woodruff went to the police, who began an investigation. Grundy's body was exhumed and examined, and was determined to contain traces of diamorphine (medical-grade heroin, legal for pain control in the UK). Shipman was arrested on 7 September 1998, and was found to own a typewriter of the type used to make the forged will.

After this, police looked at other deaths that Shipman had certified, and drew up a list of 15 specimen counts to investigate. A pattern emerged, of him overdosing patients with morphine, signing their death certificates, and then forging medical records to indicate they were in poor health.

Shipman's trial, presided over by Justice Thayne John Forbes, began on 5 October 1999. Shipman was prosecuted for the murders of Marie West, Irene Turner, Lizzie Adams, Jean Lilley, Ivy Lomas, Muriel Grimshaw, Marie Quinn, Kathleen Wagstaff, Bianka Pomfret, Naomi Nuttall, Pamela Hillier, Maureen Ward, Winifred Mellor, Joan Melia and Kathleen Grundy, over a period from 1995 to 1998.

After jury deliberations of six days, Shipman was convicted on 31 January 2000, of killing fifteen patients with lethal injections of diamorphine. The trial judge sentenced him to life imprisonment and recommended that he should never be released. In February 2002, Shipman was formally struck off the GMC register.

Shipman was one of the last prisoners to receive a government-imposed tariff. In June 2002, the Home Secretary, in accordance with the trial judge's guidance, informed Shipman that he would never leave prison. He was also convicted for forging Grundy's will, and received a four-year sentence for this.

Shipman consistently denied his guilt (his defense relying on disputing the forensic evidence against him), and never made any statements about his actions. His defense tried (and failed) to have the count of murder of Grundy, where a clear motive was alleged, tried separately from the others, where there appears to have been no strong motive.

Although there were many other cases that could have been brought to court, it was concluded that it would be hard to have a fair trial, in view of the enormous publicity surrounding the original trial; in any case, a further trial would be unnecessary, given the existing sentence. The Shipman Inquiry concluded that Shipman was probably responsible for several hundred deaths.

Some commentators have postulated that his murder of older women was somehow related to the painful experience of his mother dying when he was young, while others said the motive was an arrogant desire to control life and death. The Shipman Inquiry suggested that he liked to experiment with drugs.

It is unclear when Shipman started murdering people, or even how many he killed. A report into Shipman's activities submitted in July 2002 concluded that he had killed at least 215 of his patients between 1975 and 1998, during which time he had practised in Todmorden, West Yorkshire (1974–1975) and Hyde, Greater Manchester (1977–1998). Dame Janet Smith, the judge who submitted the report, admitted that many more suspicious deaths could not be definitively ascribed to him. Most of his victims were elderly women in good health. In total, 459 people died while under his care. It is unclear how many of these were Shipman's victims, as Shipman was often the only person to certify a death.

STEPHEN GRIFFITHS

Born
24 December 1969

Also known as:
The Crossbow Cannibal

No of victims:
3

STEPHEN SHAUN GRIFFITHS

A doctoral student, Stephen Griffiths, researching murder appeared in court Friday on charges of killing three prostitutes in northern England. He was identified when a security guard was checking tapes from the night before. Expecting to find the culprits responsible for vandalising his building the guard was shocked and horrified to find the images that would lead to the police capturing one of Britains sickest serial killers. On the tapes the guard saw a man shooting a woman with a crossbow and then removing packages from the building. Shocked, the guard called the police who swiftly led an armed raid to seize Stephen Griffiths.

Griffiths is accused of killing the three women who disappeared in Bradford, about 200 miles north of London. The 40-year-old Griffiths was studying homicide in the 19th century at the local university at the time he was arrested on the edge of the city's red-light district.

When asked to give his name in court, Griffiths said, "the crossbow cannibal." Britain's tabloid newspapers have devoted many front pages to the case and have suggested that Griffiths used a crossbow in slaying one of his victims.

When asked for his address, Griffiths shrugged and said: "Erm ... here I guess."

Relatives of some of the victims wiped away tears as they strained to see Griffiths through a glass barrier at the first of two hearings Friday. Griffiths, sporting a black shirt and dark jeans, showed little emotion, staring silently at the floor and sometimes fidgeting and touching his head.

Griffiths joined Bradford University in 2004 as a Ph.D student in local history. His research is said to focus on comparing modern policing methods with those of detectives in the 19th century.

Police said the body parts of one of his victims, 36-year-old Suzanne Blamires, were found Tuesday dumped in a nearby river. Blamires was last seen last Friday. The other two women both went missing in Bradford: Shelley Armitage, 31, disappeared since April; and Susan Rushworth, 43, has not been seen since last June.

Police were still searching the apartment complex where Griffiths lived, and forensic officers and trained dogs were combing the city for the remains of Armitage and Rushworth.

Judge James Goss adjourned the case until June 7, telling Griffiths his next appearance would be by video link to prison. Griffiths did not apply for bail.

The case has featured prominently because another serial killer had been active in the same area, the so-called "Yorkshire Ripper" serial killings of 13 women in the 1970s.

OTHER BRITISH SERIAL KILLERS

John Bodkin Adams: Was an Irish-born British general practitioner, convicted fraudster and suspected serial killer. Between the years 1946–1956, more than 160 of his patients died under suspicious circumstances.

Beverley Allitt: AKA "Angel of Death"; paediatric nurse who killed four babies in her care and injured at least nine others; sentenced to life imprisonment in 1991

Robert Black: Scottish schoolgirl killer; convicted of three murders, suspected of many more

Ian Brady and Myra Hindley: AKA "Moors Murderers"; murdered five children, aged between 10 and 17 and buried them in Saddleworth Moor

Mary Ann Britland: poisoned her daughter, husband, and the wife of her lover in 1886

William Burke and William Hare: notorious body snatchers in Edinburgh in the 19th century

George Chapman: poisoned three women; suspected by some authors of being Jack the Ripper

John Reginald Halliday Christie: killed at least six women (including his wife) between 1943 and 1953 and hid the bodies in his house. He has been implicated in the murders of one other woman and her infant child, of which Christie's fellow tenant, Timothy Evans, was convicted in 1950.

Mary Ann Cotton: British Victorian killer; said to have poisoned more than 20 victims; hanged in 1873

Thomas Neill Cream: AKA "Lambeth Poisoner"; began his killing spree in the United States then moved to London; hanged in 1892

John Duffy and David Mulcahy: AKA the "Railway Killers"; killed three women near railway stations in the 1980s

Amelia Dyer: murdered infants in her care; executed in 1896

Kenneth Erskine: AKA "Stockwell Strangler"; sentenced to life imprisonment in 1988 for murdering seven pensioners

Steven Grieveson: AKA "The Sunderland Strangler"; murdered three teenage boys in Sunderland, Tyne and Wear in 1993 and 1994

John George Haigh: AKA the "Acid Bath Murderer" and the "Vampire of London"; active in England during the 1940s; convicted of six murders, but claimed to have killed nine; executed in 1949

Archibald Hall: AKA the "Monster Butler"; killed five in

the 1970s, three with accomplice Michael Kitto

Anthony Hardy: AKA the "Camden Ripper"; convicted of three murders; suspected of at least four

Trevor Hardy: AKA "The Beast in the Night"; killed three teenage girls in Manchester from 1974 to 1976

Colin Ireland: AKA "Gay Slayer"; killed five gay men in the early 1990s

Michael Lupo: AKA "Wolf Man"; convicted of four murders and two attempted murders

Patrick Mackay: charged with the murders of five individuals, convicted of three; confessed to killing 11 people

Peter Manuel: Scottish murderer of seven, suspected of killing 15; executed in 1958

Robert Maudsley: AKA "Hannibal The Cannibal"; killer of four; killed three in prison

Peter Moore: businessman who killed four men at random in Wales

Raymond Morris: AKA the "A34 Killer"; convicted of one murder, considered to have committed at least two more

Robert Napper: AKA the "Green Chain Rapist"; killed

two women and a child in the 1990s

Donald Neilson: AKA "Black Panther"; killed four people, including heiress Lesley Whittle

Dennis Nilsen: killer of 15 (possibly 16) men between 1978 and 1983

Colin Norris: nurse convicted of killing four patients in Leeds hospitals

William Palmer: AKA "Palmer the Poisoner"; doctor suspected of numerous murders, convicted of one; hanged on June 14, 1856

Amelia Sach and Annie Walters: murdered an unknown number of babies put up for adoption

Harold Shipman AKA "Dr.Death": doctor convicted of 15 murders; a later inquiry stated he had killed at least 215 and possibly up to 457 people over a 25-year period

George Joseph Smith: AKA "The Brides in the Bath"; killer of three women

John Straffen: child killer and Britain's longest serving prisoner until his death on November 19, 2007

Peter Sutcliffe: AKA the "Yorkshire Ripper"; convicted in 1981 of murdering 13 women and attacking seven more from 1975 to 1980

Peter Tobin killer of three women

Thomas Griffiths Wainewright: artist considered to have poisoned four people

Fred West and Rosemary West: AKA "House of Horrors"; she was convicted of 10 murders; both are believed to have tortured and murdered at least 12 young women between 1967 and 1987, many at the couple's home in Gloucester; he committed suicide in 1995 while awaiting trial

Catherine Wilson: nurse considered to have poisoned seven people in the 19th century

Mary Wilson: AKA the "Merry widow of Windy Nook"; convicted of murdering two husbands by poisoning and considered to have killed two others

Steve Wright: AKA "The Suffolk Strangler" or "The Ipswich Ripper"; killed five women in six weeks around Ipswich in late 2006

Graham Young: AKA "The Teacup Poisoner"; killed three people from 1962 to 1971

CPSIA information can be obtained at www.ICGtesting.com
Printed in the USA
LVOW121556251012

304446LV00004B/172/P

9 781906 512484